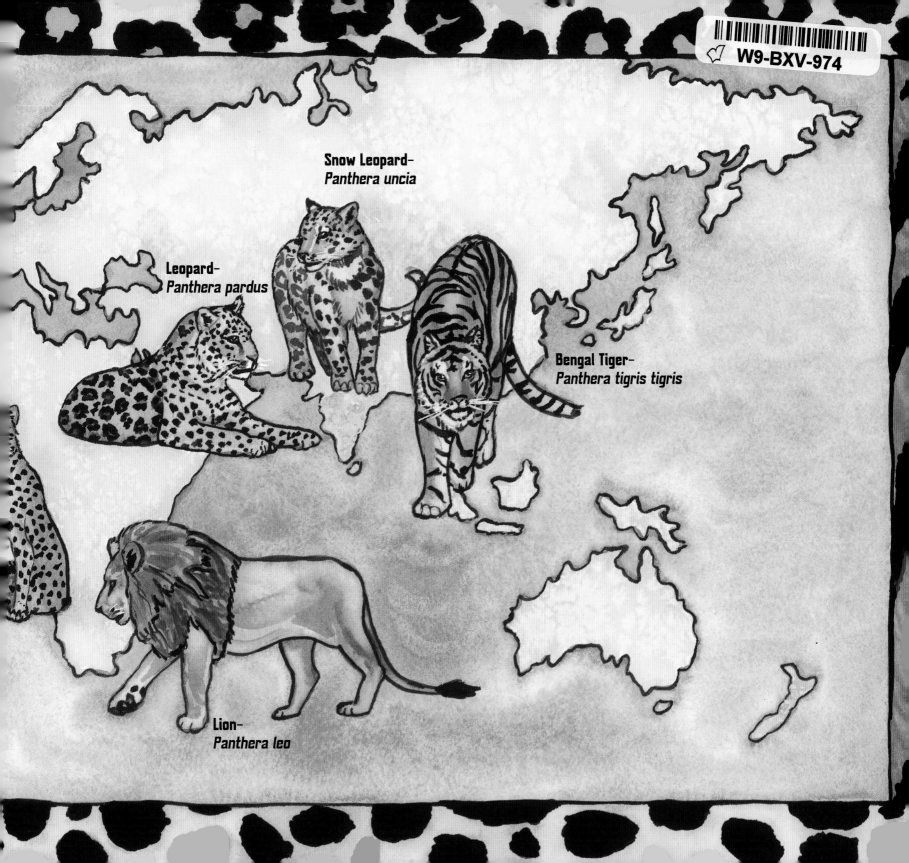

Snow Leopard–
Panthera uncia

Leopard–
Panthera pardus

Bengal Tiger–
Panthera tigris tigris

Lion–
Panthera leo

W9-BXV-974

BIG
CATS

Dorothy Hinshaw Patent

Illustrations by Kendahl Jan Jubb

WALKER & COMPANY
NEW YORK

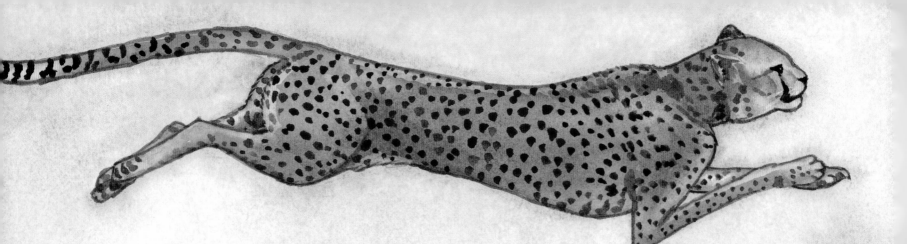

For all lovers of cats, big and small. —D. H. P.

For Otis, Oscar, Honey, and Aslan—my own "big cats." —K. J. J.

Text copyright © 2005 by Dorothy Hinshaw Patent
Illustrations copyright © 2005 by Kendahl Jan Jubb

All rights reserved. No part of this book may be reproduced or transmitted in any form or by any means, electronic or mechanical, including photocopying, recording, or by any information storage and retrieval system, without permission in writing from the Publisher.

First published in the United States of America in 2005 by Walker Publishing Company, Inc.
Distributed to the trade by Holtzbrinck Publishers

For information about permission to reproduce selections from this book, write to Permissions, Walker & Company, 104 Fifth Avenue, New York, New York 10011

Library of Congress Cataloging-in-Publication Data
available upon request

ISBN 0-8027-8968-4 (hardcover)
ISBN-13 978-0-8027-8968-6 (hardcover)
ISBN 0-8027-8969-2 (reinforced)
ISBN-13 978-0-8027-8969-3 (reinforced)
The artist used watercolors to create the illustrations for this book.

Book design by Maura Fadden Rosenthal/Mspace

Visit Walker & Company's Web site at www.walkeryoungreaders.com

Printed in Hong Kong
1 2 3 4 5 6 7 8 9 10

The big cats are among the largest, most powerful hunters on Earth. They roam through their territories in forests, grasslands, and mountains around the world in search of their prey. Big cats range in size from snow leopards and cheetahs, which weigh at most 160 pounds, to the Siberian tiger, which can weigh almost 700 pounds.

The powerful, compact bodies of big cats are designed
for hunting. Most can swim and climb trees easily. The
colors of their coats help hide them from their prey. The
stripes of a tiger and spots of a leopard or cheetah blend
in with dry grasses and with dappled light passing
through trees. The tan or grayish coat of the lion is the
same color as the dry grasslands where they usually live.
   Sometimes a black leopard or jaguar is born. The
dark color could help hide the animal in the shade of a

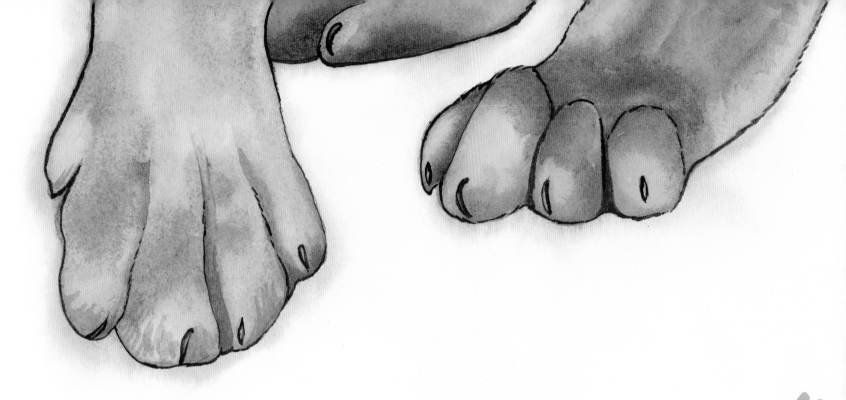

The front paws of big cats have five toes each, and the hind feet have four. The bottoms of their feet have fur between the pads, which helps soften the sound of their footsteps as they stalk their prey. Their long tails help balance their bodies during a chase.

Big cats have keen senses. Their eyes have a special layer that allows them to capture more light than human eyes. They can see six times better than we can at night. Their eyes face forward like ours, giving them binocular vision that makes it possible to judge the distances between objects well. Big cats can also see color, which helps them find their prey.

Their sensitive cup-shaped ears can turn to capture sound from different directions. Cats have long, stiff, sensitive whiskers that aid their sense of touch, helping them find their way in the dark. They also have a good sense of smell.

Most big cats hunt by silently stalking their prey, usually at night. The hunter slips silently through the bushes or grass, its body slightly crouched. When it gets near its prey, it focuses intently on one individual animal.

Then, suddenly, the cat springs into action, plunging forward to chase and leap upon its prey, grabbing it with its sharp claws and biting with its deadly jaws. But more often than not, the prey escapes unharmed, and the hungry hunter has to keep trying until it meets success.

The teeth of big cats are perfectly adapted for hunting. The front teeth, called the incisors, are small. Their largest teeth are the long, sharp canines at the front corners of the mouth. The canines are the same distance apart as the vertebrae of their most common prey. When a lion or tiger bites its prey on the back, the canines pierce between the animal's vertebrae, damaging the spinal cord so the prey is crippled. Along the sides of the mouth are sharp teeth used to slice and tear away chunks of meat.

Big cats occupy large areas of land called territories.
They use urine and special glands on their cheeks and paws to
mark trees and bushes along the borders of their territories.
For all but lions, the territory of a male is usually large and
overlaps territories of more than one female. The male will
fight another adult male that enters his territory.

Lion
Panthera leo
Head and body length: 4.7–8.2 feet
Tail length: 2.44–3.4 feet
Shoulder height: 3.5–4.2 feet
Weight of males: 330–530 pounds
Weight of females: 180–260 pounds

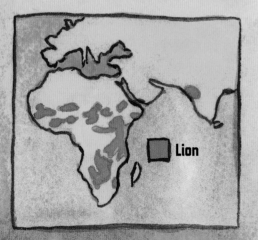

Lion

Lions are the biggest African cats. Males can weigh over five hundred pounds. That's as much as a small motorcycle. Lions now live only in Africa and a small area in Asia, but they once inhabited much of Europe, the Middle East, and northern India as well.

Lions are the only social cats. Their groups, called prides, can have more than two dozen members. The pride consists of related females, their cubs, and from one to six males. The females take care of the cubs and will nurse one another's offspring. A lioness finds a safe, hidden place when she is ready to have her cubs. As with most big cats, there are usually two to three cubs in a litter. She takes care of them by herself until they are about six weeks old. Then she introduces them to the pride.

The male lion's role is to defend the pride's territory against other lions and to fight off males that want to take over the pride. The females do most of the hunting and often work together to tackle their prey. By hunting together, lions can kill larger prey than leopards and cheetahs can. Lions have especially good eyesight. Their eyes are three times the size of human eyes and can see three times as well.

When there is enough cover from grass or bushes to hide them, lions hunt during the day. Lionesses on the prowl will secretly fan out around the prey. Then one will attack and chase it toward her hidden companions. As the prey races by, the next lioness charges and does her best to catch it.

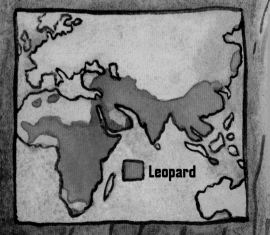

Leopard
Panthera pardus
Head and body length: 3–6.2 feet
Tail length: 2–3.8 feet
Shoulder height: 1.5–2.6 feet
Weight of males: 82–200 pounds
Weight of females: 62–135 pounds

Leopard

Leopards live throughout much of Africa and Asia. They can make their home everywhere from grasslands and deserts to forests and brush country. During the day, leopards usually rest in trees, hidden among the light and shadows of the tree leaves and branches. Leopards hunt alone, mostly at night. They hunt mostly medium-sized animals like gazelles and wildebeests, although they will also eat monkeys and baboons. When prey is scarce, leopards can survive on mice, birds, rabbits, and even insects. This powerful hunter can drag the carcass of prey heavier than itself up into a tree, where it is safe from scavengers like hyenas.

Cheetahs live throughout much of Africa except in the rain forests. They also inhabit a small area around Iran. They live in open country that has enough cover to allow them to hide while stalking their prey. Cheetahs hunt mostly during the late morning and early afternoon, when other hunters are sleeping. Even so, they are often chased from their kills by larger predators or by vultures.

Cheetah
Acinonyx jubatus
Head and body length: 3.8–5 feet
Tail length: 2–2.8 feet
Shoulder height: 2.5–3.2 feet
Weight of males: 85–130 pounds
Weight of females: 80–105 pounds

Cheetah

The cheetah's long legs, slender body, and flexible spine make it the speed champion of the world. No other land animal can run as fast—more than sixty miles an hour for a few hundred yards. Gazelles are the cheetah's favorite prey. A cheetah sneaks up to within about a hundred yards, then sprints forward, knocking over its fleeing prey and grabbing it by the throat in less than a minute. Despite the cheetah's speed, most hunts are not successful. A lone cheetah can hunt once every three to five days, but a female with cubs needs to make about one kill every day.

Siberian

Bengal

Chinese

Indochinese

Sumatran

20

Sumatran
Indochinese
Chinese
Bengal
Siberian

Tiger
Panthera tigris
Head and body length: 4.7–9.5 feet
Tail length: 2–3.8 feet
Shoulder height: 2.7–3.8 feet
Weight of males: 200–680 pounds
Weight of females: 145–360 pounds

Tigers are by far the biggest of the big cats. A large male tiger outweighs a big male lion by 150 pounds. There are actually five surviving types, or subspecies, of tiger pictured above from left to right: the Sumatran, Indochinese, Bengal, Chinese, and Siberian. Sumatran males weigh as much as 300 pounds, the size of a professional football player.

Siberian males can weigh 680 pounds and measure more than thirteen feet from the tip of the nose to the tip of the tail. That's as long as a compact car!

Tigers live in Asia, from the bitter cold of Siberia to the hot, humid tropics, where daytime temperatures regularly reach more than 100 degrees Fahrenheit during the heat of the day. When it gets really hot, tigers will take a dip in a pond or stream to help cool off.

Because of its great size and strength, a tiger can bring down prey much larger than itself, such as the wild cattle called gaur. The chital, or axis deer, is a favorite food in India, while Siberian tigers favor wild boar. A tiger gorging on a carcass can eat seventy or more pounds of food at one time. Tigers spend a lot of time hunting, making a kill about every three days. Only about one hunt in ten is successful.

Of the big cats, the tiger is the most dangerous to people. Few tigers stalk human prey, but just one man-eater can terrorize an entire village. Tigers have been slaughtered in huge numbers by people, partly because of the threat they can pose and partly because their bones and pelts are very valuable. Thanks to international cooperation, trade in tiger pelts has gone down. But in Asia, tiger bones are still thought to help cure diseases and bring strength when consumed in pills, liquid medicine, or wine.

The snow leopard is the most mysterious of big cats, for its habitat is so rough and rugged few people share its home. It lives in the Himalayan mountains, usually at altitudes of over a mile above sea level. Its beautiful grayish spotted coat helps hide it among snow-blotched rocks. Its three-foot-long tail is covered with thick fur and can be tucked around its face to protect it from the cold.

Snow Leopard
Panthera uncia
Head and body length: 3.5–4.5 feet
Tail length: 2.7–3.5 feet
Shoulder height: about 2 feet
Weight of males: 100–120 pounds
Weight of females: 80–100 pounds

☐ Snow Leopard

Snow leopards hunt during the early morning and late afternoon, stalking or ambushing their prey. They eat whatever they can catch, from small animals such as pikas, which weigh less than a pound, to large ones such as Asian mountain goats and deer.

25

The most familiar big cat in North America is the cougar, or mountain lion. It can be found from coast to coast and from parts of Canada southward, deep into South America. Cougars live in just about any habitat, from cold, northern pine forests to hot, tropical rain forests. They thrive in brushlands and deserts, in swamps and grasslands.

Cougar
Felis concolor
Head and body length: 3.4–6.3 feet
Tail length: 1.9–2.8 feet
Shoulder height: 2–2.4 feet
Weight of males: 150–235 pounds
Weight of females: 80–130 pounds

Cougar

Cougars are actually more closely related to house cats than they are to jaguars and tigers. But they are about the same size as leopards, so they qualify as big cats. Their color ranges from shades of reddish tan to shades of gray, with a lighter belly. Their favorite prey is deer, although they also eat other prey, such as beavers, hares, and wild hogs.

Jaguar
Panthera onca
Head and body length: 3.2–6.2 feet
Tail length: 1.5–2.6 feet
Shoulder height: 2–3 feet
Weight of males: 120–275 pounds
Weight of females: 100–200 pounds

Jaguar

Jaguars live in tropical parts of the Americas. They share much of their habitat with cougars. They once lived in what is now Arizona, but today they are found in most of South and Central America and as far north as Mexico. Jaguars rarely leave the dense forest. They hunt by ambushing or stalking their prey. They are very strong, with especially thick, muscular necks and shoulders. They climb and swim well and feed on more than eighty-five different kinds of animals, from mice and fish to deer and monkeys.

Jaguars have been hunted mercilessly. During the 1960s, fifteen thousand jaguars were killed each year just in Brazil. Their homes have been logged and burned, too, to the point that they now survive only in isolated pockets of forest. Altogether, 1.5 billion acres where jaguars once lived have been taken over by humans for farms, roads, and towns.

30

Most big cats have beautiful fur that is highly valued in many cultures. Sometimes they attack humans and their livestock. They also require large areas of wildlands in order to have enough space to hunt and reproduce. For all these reasons, the survival of big cats is often at odds with the needs of the ever-growing human population on Earth.

Jaguars aren't the only big cats in trouble today. Both the tiger and the snow leopard are endangered species. This means that if people don't work hard to protect them and their habitats, these magnificent animals could easily disappear forever. The Siberian tiger is critically endangered, meaning its survival in the wild is especially doubtful.

The other big cats are also at risk. Only the leopard and cougar seem to manage to survive well today, and both of them have disappeared from much of their original range. While lions live on many preserves in Africa, the Asiatic lion is critically endangered, with only about two hundred surviving in the wild. Cheetahs and jaguars could both be placed on the endangered species list in the future, unless efforts to protect them and their homes are continued.

Index of Big Cats in This Book
(with scientific names)

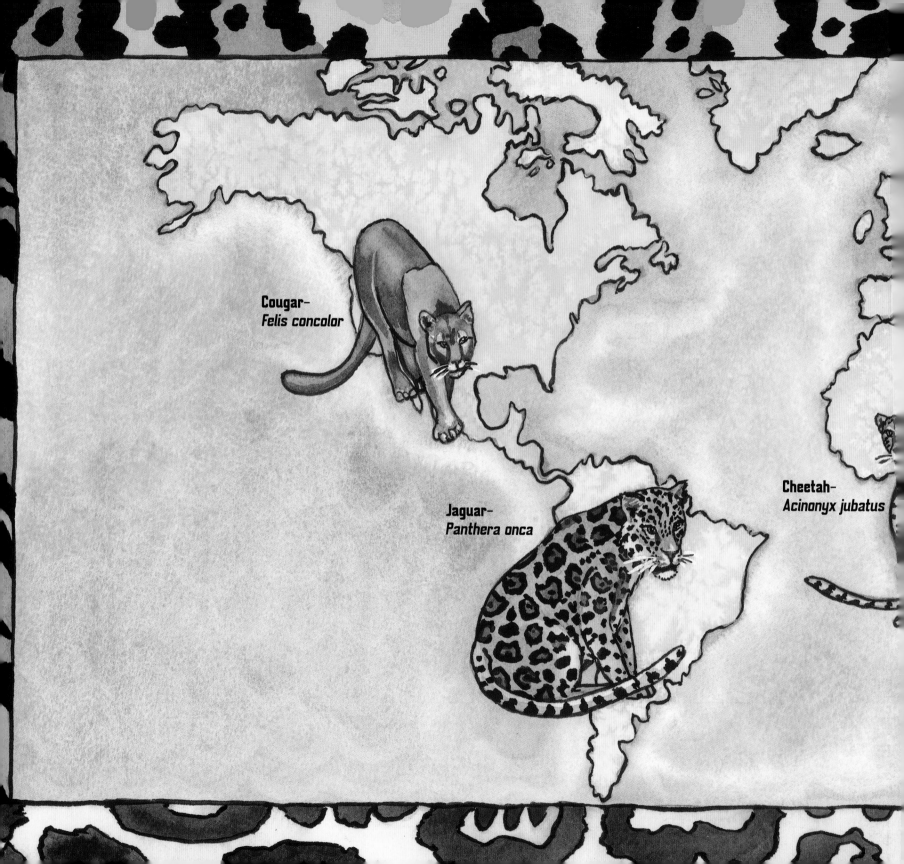

Cougar–
Felis concolor

Jaguar–
Panthera onca

Cheetah–
Acinonyx jubatus